How To Teach Kids To Be MILLIONAIRES

How To Teach

Kids To Be

MILLIONAIRES

By: Cuttie W. Bacon, III, Ph.D.
Co-authored by: Cuttie W. Bacon, IV, MBA

Published by:
Dr. Knose Publications
Chicago, Illinois

How To Teach Kids To Be Millionaires
By: Cuttie W. Bacon, III, Ph.D.
Co-authored by: Cuttie W. Bacon, IV, MBA

Copyright © MM

Published by: Dr. Knose Publications, Chicago Illinois

Cover Design and Page Layout by: Ad Graphics, Tulsa, OK

Printed in the United States of America

ISBN Number: 0-9678544-1-5

About the Author

Cuttie Bacon was born in Western Kentucky and lived the first four years of his life on a farm where his Father was a farmer. Cuttie Bacon grew up in Louisville, Kentucky where he finished high school and graduated from Kentucky State University. He moved to Chicago where he earned a Master's Degree at Loyola University in Chicago and a Ph.D. at Northwestern University in Evanston, Illinois. Cuttie has taught at Northwestern University, Mundelein College, Governors State University, National College and has led numerous seminars over the past twenty years. His administrative experience in public school started as a Principal and later as a Superintendent of Schools in the Southern Suburbs of Chicago.

Cuttie belongs to more than twenty national organizations, but is most proud of his membership and Professional Speakers Certification with the National Association of African American Speakers; Chicago Chapter. He frequently speaks on "How to Cut Your Income Tax," "How to Live a Rich and Prosperous Life," "How to Write Your Own Book," and numerous educational topics.

He is presently co-authoring two books. One with his brother about *"How to Stay out of the Correctional System"* and his second book on *"Awareness, Prevention and Survival of Prostrate Cancer for African American Males."*

Cuttie is an entertaining speaker and is able to see the humorous side of life in almost any subject. Among his many hobbies is restoring exotic and antique cars.

Cuttie consistently speaks on prosperity conscience and how to enjoy the rich life. His company is Dr. Knose Seminars; email him at:

Cuttie3@Compuserve.com

or call toll free, 1-800-995-9934.

Foreword

Teaching kids to be millionaires is strongly needed in our society today. Whether it is a household with a $10,000/year income or $1,000,000/year income, my experience for the last 35 years has made it crystal clear that adults need "how to" information to properly teach personal finances to children of all ages. In a recent meeting with more than 300 parents and guardians, I was encouraged to write this book and recommend it to all adults who are involved directly or indirectly with children today.

Acknowledgments

To acknowledge all of the sources I consulted with in preparing this book would be impossible with the space I have. To acknowledge every source would probably require 3 or 4 pages. The inspiration in writing this book was supplied by my first born granddaughter who has frequently, in her 11 years, attempted to explain to me why she always asked me for $10-20 and why she could not invest any portion of the money she received from me. Significant encouragement has come from my son, Cuttie W. Bacon IV; the co-author of this book and my daughter Cutia Bacon-Brown; my first born.

I sincerely thank all of the people who encouraged and assisted me and always pushed me through to completion.

A Word from the Author

I sincerely appreciate you taking the time and investing the money to allow me to share some of my concepts with you. I have been a teacher, Professor, Principal and School Superintendent for more than 35 years of my life and feel a strong commitment to children and parents and a commitment to writing self-help books for parents and guardians. I believe every child has the potential of acquiring huge sums of wealth through the assistance and education of adults in their lives. Please use this book to make certain children in your life develop wealth. Starting today!

Table of Contents

Table of Contents

The lack of money
can be the root of evil.

– Cuttie Bacon

Introduction

For more that 20 years I have taught from kindergarten through graduate school. I have found that with few exceptions, 95% of the children and young adults I have encountered know little if anything about money management. I have taught personal finance, economics, entrepreneurship and mathematics. After teaching thousands of students, I have concluded that our only hope of teaching sound money management practices is to teach parents and encourage parents to teach children. After talking to many of the parents of children I have taught, I have found that almost none of the parents that I have encountered feel they know enough about money, money management, and investment to be able to teach their children. Some parents say they plan to talk to their children about money, but generally that talk ends up like their plans to talk to their children about sex – they just don't get around to it or don't know what to say to their children.

Over the last 37 years, my children have given me an incredible education in what youngsters think about the purpose of money. I find that my teaching techniques are far better with my grandchildren than they were with my children. After wasting thousands of dollars, I now know how to invest, how to spend, and how to teach my children to guide my grandchildren's spending and investing.

Children hear references to preserving money generally from 2 years old until they leave home. Most of the time they hear things like:

> *"Turn the water hose off! The water bill*
> *is going to be a million dollars!"*

Chapter 1

Investing Money for Your Child from Birth to 3 Years Old

Investing for your child is one of the most important things you will do with money that you can also share with your child. I advise adults to put in their budget $1 - $2 per day to be deposited in their child's piggy bank from the day the child is born until that child is 21. Putting $1 or $2 a day into a child's piggy bank will allow you (at the end of each month) to deposit a minimum of $30 into a checking account and open a mutual fund for your child.

It is crucial to make the $1 to $2 investment from the day the child is born so that this becomes a habit for you and your family.

Investing a dollar a day
will keep poverty far away.

– Cuttie W. Bacon, III

Where to get the $1 - $2 per day

The average person probably spends at least $1,000 a year on clothing, toys and gifts for their child. They spend this primarily out of emotion. Most parents understandably want their children dressed in cute little outfits. Some even believe this is a must. I believe that you can cut your budget for toys, clothing and non-essentials and invest $1 or $2 a day for your child. You must keep in mind that until around 4 years of age, your child has no real knowledge of what he or she is wearing, what it cost, and certainly what brand it is. This is a perfect time to make maximum investments that will lead to accumulating wealth for your child.

Some parents recruit clothing from relatives and friends the first 3 or 4 years of their child's life and thereby substantially reduce spending on clothing. Others use better thrift stores where most items cost $1 to $2 each and limit their yearly cost to $300 or less. It is possible for the first 4 years of a child's life to spend $200 or less for your child through thrift store purchases and gifts from family members or friends.

Spending $200 or less for your child allows the average family approximately $750 to be invested in the child's future.

Throughout this book I will focus on limiting spending and economical spending so that your budget will allow $2 per day for 21 years which will amount to a minimum of $730 per year for investments. Investing $730 per year for 21 years at an average of 15% interest will amount to more than $200,000 in 21 years.

Investing vs. Savings Accounts

Throughout this book you will notice my primary focus will be on investing as opposed to saving. Traditional savings accounts do not offer the growth potential that investments in mutual funds, stocks and other investment instruments offer. Many people will argue that secure savings accounts and insurance will guarantee certain amounts of money. I do not disagree with the idea of having guaranteed amounts of money, however, my focus is on the money that you invest for your child, especially after 3 years old, will often be in the form of junk food and fast food. This is essentially throw away money. This is money that is thrown away. You'll never see it nor its dividends after it is "invested" in the candy, junk food, or fast food. Any level of risk associated with money that will be thrown away in junk food and candy can withstand any loss from investment. You can be certain that you will get no return on the junk food investment, but you can expect with some probability you will get 10% or more on your long term investment.

A friend of mine whose child is 15 years old has used a similar investment plan and is now investing in high risk securities in the amount of $750 per day. He now has in excess of $200,000 of which he invests annually $100,000. He says if he loses $100,000 it is only money that would have been thrown away on candy and fast foods anyway.

Additional monies that may be available to you for investment ages 1-3

It is customary that when a child is born, grandparents, godparents, uncles, aunts and other relatives and friends feel obligated to bring gifts for birthdays, Christmas, and other occasions. Some child psychologists believe that from birth to 3 years old, large numbers of gifts and toys are not necessary for most kids. This is a time that parents and guardians can capitalize on the gift giving traditions and request that relatives and friends give money or saving instruments that can be converted into investments and other securities for the child.

In discussing gifts and the cost of gifts from relatives and friends with several parents and others, I was amazed to find that children from 1 to 3 years old on the average were receiving in excess of $500 in toys, gifts and clothing throughout the year. If these gifts could be converted into money for investments for the child, a parent would be able to invest $1,000 per year for a child starting at birth, and $1,000 per year for 21 years. At some of the interest rates we have experienced in the late 90's a child could have more than a quarter of a million dollars.

Chapter 2

How to Spend Money

Generally when we discuss money as adults, one of the very first things we talk about is how to save money. A great deal of time and energy is allotted to saving money because saving for most American adults is a dreadfully difficult challenge. Only a small percentage of Americans can consistently save 10% of their income. So when adults discuss money management with children, we often spend a considerable amount of time encouraging them to do what we can't do, and that is to save. I do not disagree with the philosophy of saving, but I do believe that it is considerably more important to teach our children how to spend money. Teaching our children how to spend money and when to spend should start somewhere between

2 and 3 years old. Most American youth will begin to ask for money somewhere between 2 and 3 years old. Their requests for money at those ages are often to buy candy, junk food, and toys. Parents and guardians are solely responsible for introducing and supplying candies, food, and toys to children at such a young and tender age. Most of our youngsters decide the kind of candy, junk food and toys they want based on television and what they are exposed to by adults and children around them.

Most of us are aware of the negative effect of sugar based snacks and candies on our children. Consequently, our first lesson to children in spending should be why they should not purchase, and why you are not going to allow them funds to purchase items such as candy and junk foods with their high content of sugar. The following are reasons why you should educate your youngsters and deny them high sugar content candy and snacks.

Reason 1:   Candy destroys teeth.

Reason 2:   For many kids candy elevates their level of hyperactivity.

Reason 3:   There are no returns on this investment.

Reason 4:   It often ruins the child's appetite for healthy food.

For the above reasons, part of the spending education for youngsters starting at 2 and up is,

Thou shalt not have nor buy candy or items with a high sugar content.

At age 3 – 6 more than 75% of the money youngsters spend are on candy and junk food. You can teach your child that 50% of the money they get will go to a piggy bank to be invested at the end of the month. As the child grows older, you will experience many more challenges and questions about money and the child's ability to decide what he wants to do with money. These are opportune times to continue to educate him or her on no candy, junk foods, and junk toys. As the requests grow more numerous for money, it is time to decide what chores your child must do to earn money.

Payroll vs. allowance for children 3 years and up

I advocate payrolls rather than allowance for children once they are old enough to ask for money. By payroll I mean EARNED WAGES. Childhood experiences with money should be directly related to life experiences. As an adult who has worked more than 55 years in my life, no one ever gave me money. Money was earned from work or dividends from investing in securities or wages earned from performing services. The same should be for children over the age of 3.

Jobs a 3 year old or older could do

In a child's room every item such as shoes, toys and books should have a specific place. It is a child's duty twice a day to make sure that everything is in its designated place, preferably at the end of the day and midday which can easily to be tied to naptime and bedtime. How he or she should be taken through the routine of putting items in their designated place twice a day and be advised of an amount of compensation that he or she will receive for performance of his or her duties.

These kinds of activities and others can be the first step in arranging for payroll for a child from age 3-6.

Earning what we traditionally call an allowance provides a youngster with a life experience that will be carried to adulthood. That life experience is,

Money is directly related to the amount of services you render.

Teaching children to earn money by working reinforces adult values and trains a child to understand that money is acquired through work effort. When children earn money from providing services they no longer relate receiving money as a gift with expecting more gifts, which makes it much easier to spend money or give it away. When a child has to put forth a work effort for money, he sees a relationship between work and money. As a child grows older from 3 – 9 years, you have to continuously develop additional jobs with a higher degree of difficulty for him or her to earn money. These jobs may be taking out the garbage, bringing in the paper, organizing and putting toys where they should be, and various household duties such as cleaning their own room,

Spending money can be insane,
investing money is never in vain.

– Cuttie W. Bacon, III

cleaning the bathroom and running errands to the store and other places.

Continuously finding jobs for a child to do and attaching rates of pay to these jobs allows parents to pay a child for a job rather than giving him an allowance.

How to Spend Money

How to spend money continues to be the number one priority to teach children. No matter how well you teach them to invest money they may go out and spend it on foolish items. First lets look at two of the most influential items in our society that have an effect on how children spend their money. Most of our children spend a considerable number of hours a day watching television. Television ads are one of the strongest influences on spending. Today from birth through adulthood we are told over and over again what we should buy. My granddaughter taught me at 3 years old that she was very clear on what foods she liked. She informed me that for lunch, dinner, and breakfast she only ate MickieD's food. When I attempted to persuade her to trying other foods and other restaurants she insisted that other foods were no good and she always had to have a Kiddy Meal, cheeseburger, french fries, pie, or shake from MickieD's.

After becoming very frustrated with this response to food, I decided to change her eating habits. During a one-week vacation with me, I decided that I was not going to purchase any products from MickieD's. At first I was met with great resistance, but by evening, her hunger reached a level that she could not stand anymore and she decided to eat my cooking. Being happy about my success, I insisted on her eating different foods the whole week, but had to insure her that she would receive a monetary reward for doing such.

I am convinced that adults can change the eating habits of youngsters and can use the money spent on junk foods and candy to invest for children at the rate of 2-3 sometimes as much as $5 per day. Over a span of 21 years a youngster can accumulate more than a half million dollars.

Today, game companies, through television ads, have produced the same or similar effect on our children. High tech toys and games now cost between $20 - $300. It is not uncommon to find children in moderate income families who own $5 - $600 worth of high tech toys. These toys are found interesting only as long as they are advertised on television. Frequently changing the toys that are advertised on television arouses our children to want the new toys and consequently throw aside toys they have had for a month or two. This is another area of spending that can be reduced by 90%. The money could be used to assist children in becoming wealthy adults.

Designer clothing and designer sneakers are frequently advertised on television. Parents today are spending billions of dollars at the insistence of their children due to television advertisements. Surveying several parents, I found that it is common for parents to buy 4-6 pair of designer sneakers per year at a cost of sometimes higher than $100 per pair. Many designer jackets, jeans, caps and other clothing items sell for over $100. Many parents spend in excess of 2-3 thousand dollars per year on clothing items that quickly go out of style due to television advertisements. The following shows a summary of unwise spending.

Unwise Spending Chart

1.   Junk food. Average spending $3 per day, 365 days per year – $1,095/year.

2.   Candy. $2 per day – $730 per year.

3.   Designer clothing. $200 per month – $2,400 per year.

4.   Miscellaneous money given to children. $1 per day – $365 per year.

        Total: $5,090 per year

This is over $5,000 that could be invested in the child's future. At this rate, if invested at a rate of 12% in 21 years, the child would have accumulated wealth in excess of a half million dollars.

The next chart shows typical spending for a household with an income of $40,000 or less per year. If spending was seriously examined and was followed with a wise spending chart, it would look like this.

Wise Spending Chart

1. Junk food – zero dollars spent.

2. Healthy snacks. Fifty cents per day, approximately $180 per year.

3. High tech toys. 1 toy per year – $50.

4. Designer sneakers. Zero dollars per year. Generic shoes – 4 pair at $160 per year.

5. Designer clothing. Zero dollars spent. Non-designer clothing – $50 per month at $600 per year.

As you can see the difference in the two charts of unwise and wise spending for a child is approximately $3,000. That is $3,000 that could be invested at 15% or more per year. For 21 years it would accumulate to approximately $380,000.

Most would agree that this is an excellent graduation present for any college graduate. It allows financial freedom not often associated with recent graduates.

Money grows too slow
in savings accounts.

– Cuttie W. Bacon, III

Chapter 3

How Money Grows

Probably since the beginning of time, parents have told children that money does not grow on trees. We often forget and sometimes don't know how to teach children the way money grows. Money grows in many ways, but the number one rule to remember in explaining how money grows is the Rule of 72. The Rule of 72 illustrates how long it will take for an investment to double. Divide the number 72 by the rate of interest that an investment pays to find the number of years it will take to double the initial investment. For example: if you are earning 12 percent on your investment, it will take 6 years for your money to double. You will find that by diving 12 into 72 (and that is using the compound interest theory) compound interest is interest that is figured on all monies in the account including any prior interest that has been earned.

There is great controversy over when we should begin to teach children how money grows.

Your money will grow if you plant it in the right account.

– Cuttie W. Bacon, III

I believe that you can teach children how money grows. I believe that you can teach children how money grows as soon as they are old enough to ask for money. Rule 72 may be a little complicated for a 3 year old, but as it is explained from 6 years old to 9 years, I believe the child can comprehend it and comprehend it well after 9 years old.

Investing $3 per day for your child for 15 years will amount to more than $50,000 at 15% and investing $1,000 per year for 21 years will amount to more than $138,000. Investing $42 two times per month will equal more than $1,000 per year for your child. This is accomplished with as little as $3-4 invested per day.

This illustrates why we have millions of young adults who should have a half million dollars or more in a portfolio but have no money in a portfolio because they have not been taught how to correctly spend their money. This further emphasizes why I believe it is crucial to teach our children how to spend and consequently how to invest their money to accumulate wealth.

Start a home based business
so your children can learn
while they earn.

– Cuttie W. Bacon, III

Chapter 4

Home Based Businesses that Children Can Run

B y the age of six, most children are sophisticated enough to run their own home-based businesses with the help of an adult, of course. The following is a list of businesses that I have observed children aged 6 – 12 years manage with great success and minimal adult supervision.

- Greeting Card Businesses
- Healthy Soap Manufacturing
- School Supplies
- Candy Stores
- Sports Trading Cards
- Resale Toy Stores
- High Tech Toy Trading Stores

- Cookie Manufacturers

- Candle Manufacturers

- Shoeshine

- Lemonade

- Ice-cream

- Pizzas

- Peanuts

- Popcorn

- Flyer Design and Distribution

- Bicycle Repairs

- Errand Running Services

- Pet Sitting

- Car Wash

- Senior Companions

- Peer Tutoring

- Balloon Businesses

I have observed children 6 years old and older involved in all of these businesses. I recommend that these endeavors be custodial or headed by adults 21 years or older because some of these businesses require contracts which cannot be executed by minors. Most all of the other functions of these businesses can be executed by children with great success.

One of the most interesting businesses I have encountered was when my god sons operated a Flyer Distribution company. At less than 12 years old, they were producing on computer and distributing enough flyers to net $150 per week. As a part-time business with minimal assistance this business had the potential of grossing $300 per week.

To assist youngsters in growing wealth with a business that produces $150 per week, a child's parent or guardian needs to make absolutely clear that no less than 75% of the profits will be invested for the child. Investing $100 or more per week for a child at 15% or more per year will allow the child to have more than a million dollars in 25 years.

The steps in assisting a child in organizing a business and making a profit in order to have substantial wealth by the time that he is an adult involves a simple business plan.

Home based businesses are the fastest growing businesses in the US. Don't delay, start today.

– Cuttie W. Bacon, III

Assisting children in starting their own businesses is the first step in introducing them to entrepreneurship and how economic systems work. It is crucial in the 21st century to give children an early introduction to owning their own businesses and understanding how to accumulate wealth. This gives them an understanding of how millions and billions are earned in the world. It is also crucial for youngsters to understand the need to own their own business and manufacture their own goods because the job market as we knew it in the 20th century will not exist. No longer can an individual work for one company for 25 years and retire. Due to downsizing and our global economy it is my belief that the only truly dependable career for our children is a career of self-employment.

It's never too late to teach
children how to spend.

— Cuttie W. Bacon, III

Chapter 5

Teaching Kids How to Spend Their Money

A money spending plan is commonly known as a budget. Many times adults are reluctant to attempt to teach children how to live on a budget because most adults find it difficult, if not impossible to live on a budget. The reason a child must have a budget is because the money that he or she is receiving from you, a part-time job, his or her business, and any other money from gifts, must be accounted for, and as we stated in previous chapters, must be spent wisely. When to begin a budget is a decision that a parent must make. However, I suggest that it is never too early to start a money spending plan with a child. It is never too late to start if you have neglected it for the first few years of a child's life.

Starting a budget plan is very simple. Start it when your child asks for his first 5 cents. Start by explaining to your child where the money will come from, how much he or she is going to get, and what he or she must do to get the money. If your decision for a 3 year old is 50 cents per week, explain to him or her what will be received and what will happen if he spends the total amount. Do not give additional monies after he or she spends the amount you have allotted for that week.

As your child approaches 5 years of age or when he is old enough to count to 100, explain what a dollar is and how many pennies, nickels, dimes and quarters are contained within a dollar. Approximately 5-6 years is an appropriate time to make a list of everything your child wants and needs at that age. Make a list of toys, games, candy, snacks, school lunch, movies, clothing, and personal needs. Explain to your child what you pay for these items what they cost. Explain to your child what he or she must buy with the money you give him or her and what must be done without if money is misappropriated. Have your child make a weekly budget and a weekly spending list. At the end of the week, make sure you go over your child's budget with him and try to hold him accountable for all expenditures as well as what he has kept. As your child grows older, his budget can grow in sophistication. In time, begin to explain family budgets and finances with your child to assist in understanding how money is managed in the household and how it relates to him or her. At this point, allow your child to do a budget for himself. This is an experience that every child should have. Allow your child to tell you (out of their business or paycheck) what they need to spend out of that business or paycheck and why. Insist on a portion for saving and investing. Check your child's budget to make certain that the amount they plan to spend does not exceed their income. Make certain that included in their spending is a portion for investing and insist that it is invested on a weekly basis. There are certain amounts that remain the same. These amounts may be school lunch, investment amounts, church donations and other fixed expenses. You may help your child in identifying week-to-week, and month-to-month variable costs.

It is a good concept to keep the investment amount consistent with the child's income and teach the child the habit of paying themselves first. The concept of paying themselves involves investing their money and watching it grow. Advise your child that as their income increases or de-

Most people do not fail
to manage their money,
most people fail to have a
good money spending plan
that they follow.

– Cuttie W. Bacon

creases during the year, they may need to revise their budget, or at the start of every semester, change or revise their budget.

Insisting that your child keep a spending notebook is crucial. A small notebook with every date of the month included will suffice. Record every penny they spend per day. This allows you to assist your child in evaluating his or her spending habits and look for ways to invest more money in their business or better plan their budgets.

Several advantages of teaching children budgets at a young age is it allows your youngster to plan their savings and investment program at a young age. A budget allows your child to invest and save money that he or she did not expect to receive. A budget allows a child to set financial goals that assist them in structuring and organizing their spending. A budget allows your child to know the amount of money he has coming in and how to keep track of it. A budget assists your child in planing to have the money they need for things they want to do.

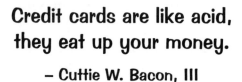

Credit cards are like acid,
they eat up your money.

– Cuttie W. Bacon, III

Chapter 6

Never Use Credit Cards

How to invest the interest you would pay on credit cards

One of the greatest rip-offs in America today is the interest that is being charged on charge cards. If you calculate what you pay on a typical charge card you would find some shocking information. A person who charges $3,000 on a credit card typically pays a rate of at least 20%. In addition to the 20% or more, people are paying $30 or more as an annual fee for the "privilege" of paying this exorbitant rate of interest.

If you calculate what you pay to a company when you charge $3,000 on your card, you will find that if you make only the minimum monthly payment, you will pay more than $12,000 in finance charges alone. It will take you more than 9 years to pay back the $3,000 even if you make every payment on time. Why does it take so long? It takes so long because some companies require you to pay less than $60 dollars per month and only a very small portion of the $60 goes on toward the principal.

Most Americans keep at least two credit cards and never pay them off in full. So to reverse this trend, my recommendation is that you use credit cards only when you can pay the balance in full in 30 days. Furthermore, train and teach your children never to use credit cards and show them how much money they would have if they invested the interest in an annuity or an IRA account. For example, if your child invested as little as $2,000 per month for approximately 30 years earning at least 15% per year, he would have approximately a half million dollars.

Since most people have charge accounts and pay at least $2,000 per year for 50 years, if they invested this amount for 50 years in an account earning at least 15%, they would have approximately 3 million dollars.

The moral of the story is never, never, never, charge and pay on an account year after year. In a lifetime you are giving away millions of dollars which you will never get back.

In teaching your child how to be a millionaire, show him how dreadful purchasing on credit cards is and the amount of money you actually pay for an item when you charge such small amounts. Avoid charging in front of your child. Make a plan to stop charging because when you tell your child you do not have money, they will encourage you to use a credit card. Use this time as an opportunity to teach your child the dangers of using credit cards. Also use these occasions to give him or her a list of companies and businesses who charge ridiculously high amounts. Remember, many of your popular name department stores, sporting goods stores, toy stores, clothing stores, and where they have credit accounts easily available for you frequently will advertise on the Internet. They tell you to just call in and shop and charge high amounts of 19-23% or more. Show your children how ridiculously high these amounts are and on such small amounts as $1,000, you will end up paying back as much as $4,000 in finance charges even if you make all the payments on time.

It is easy to use a credit card
but so hard to make
the payments.

– Cuttie W. Bacon, III

These are crucial lessons to teach children. Far too many children are exposed to and encouraged to charge on their parent's charge accounts on e-commerce and other easy purchasing gimmicks online. Also, these are great times to teach the child how he or she can earn interest using stocks and bonds, savings accounts, certificates of deposit and many other investment instruments rather than pay interest.

Many people ask at what age you should begin teaching children about credit cards and high interest rates. I believe you should teach your children about credit cards and high interest rates as soon as they are old enough to know what a credit card is. For many youngsters this is as early as 5 years old.

For additional information, please send $5.00 for our booklet on *How to Stay Away from Credit Cards and High Interest Accounts*.

Call: 1-800-955-9934.

Money is not everything,
but it will allow you to
purchase most things.

– Cuttie W. Bacon, III

Chapter 7

Mutual Funds for Children

A Mutual Fund is where a large group puts their money into a company and the company invests the money in any of a number of different types of securities. The money is managed by sound financial professionals. Example: ten bankers get together and create ABC Kids Mutual Fund. One million children invest $10. ABC Mutual Fund would then have 10 million dollars and would invest the money in various stocks or bonds and manage these stocks for the one million children that invested. When the stocks makes a dividend of a million dollars, the company may decide to pay each child that invested a share of 50 cents. That is the way investments are made and dividends are distributed in a Mutual Fund company. Ten men may very well be the managers of the ABC Fund for the children.

Mutual Funds are an excellent way to get your child started in investing. Mutual Funds do not require extensive knowledge of the stock market. Many Mutual Fund companies today have investment information for children. Mutual Funds today are very popular and it is a way that children can own a portion of Corporate America. Instead of buying shares of stock from a particular company, a child can buy shares in a Mutual Fund and the Mutual Fund buys shares in individual stocks. Among some of the benefits of purchasing Mutual Funds are an investor can pull his money out any time he desires. Keep in mind, like stocks, there are no guarantees that you can get out what you put in. You are however, able to draw out the cash value at any time.

Probably the most attractive feature of investing in Mutual Funds is that these funds are managed by well-trained, skillful money managers. Mutual Fund managers have extensive experience in knowing what stocks or bonds to buy, what stock to sell, when to buy certain stocks and many of the investment techniques that amateurs do not know.

Purchasing shares of a Mutual Fund can be done with as little as $20 per month. The big question is how do you make money in Mutual Funds? One way is dividends. When the fund collect dividends on the stock it owns, it passes these profits on to investors in the fund. In other words, when the stock market goes up, and the Mutual Fund owns a number of the stocks that increase in price and dividends are collected, these dividends are passed on to the people who own shares in the Mutual Fund.

Capital Gains

Mutual Funds may earn money when they sell stocks. When this happens the gains are sometimes passed on to investors in the form of capital gains distribution.

Capital Gains from Selling Fund Shares

When a child owns shares of a Mutual Fund and the shares increase in value, a child may sell through his custodian his shares at a profit and have capital gains. You must also keep in mind that Mutual Funds do not always earn money. When stocks drop in price and shares in a com-

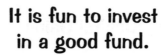

It is fun to invest
in a good fund.

– Cuttie W. Bacon, III

pany decrease, the value of Mutual Funds may drop. There are no guarantees ever of earning money. However, most Mutual Funds in a long period of time have earned money.

The following is an example of earning large amounts over a period of time in Mutual Funds:

$1,000/month for 10 years @25% = $482,140

$1,000/month for 5 years @25% = $119,273

$500/month for 10 years @25%= $241,069

$250/month for 5 years @25% - $29,818

There are a number of companies who are catering to children to invest in Mutual Funds today. For your child to invest in Mutual Funds, the investment must be made in a custodial account. A custodial account is designed for all minors. An adult would have to sign contracts. Some of these funds target children. They target children and hopefully get them in a habit of investing so that when they become adults they are already customers of these companies.

Many funds have material written at primary school reading levels so that youngsters as young as 6 years can read and understand. Some have newsletters and other materials written at an understanding level tailored for children. Many of these companies have no restrictions for investments – only that minors have a custodian. Many of the stocks that companies run like this would be that youngsters would be buying their products such as candy companies, chewing gum companies, and sports companies. Their materials provide information to children that can be easily read. Easily understood stock market information is also provided for children.

Minimum amounts required by these companies to invest per month can range from $20 and up. For your child to join you simply have to complete an application or have your child complete the application. Be sure to have the signature of the custodian on all paperwork. This can also be done online. It is a simple process. For example, if you want to join and buy shares in ABC Kids Mutual Fund you would simply complete the application, sign the account and mail a check to get started. Information would be sent to you on your account. Quarterly Reports would be sent to you detailing how your Mutual Fund is doing.

When dividends on capital gains are paid, you will have the option of receiving a check for your child's account. You may decide to reinvest the money. I recommend that you reinvest the fund so that the monies earned can earn additional money very much like you earn money in a compound interest account.

For additional information on many of the characteristics of Mutual Funds and stocks, call 1-800-955-9934 for ordering information for additional information and booklets on Mutual Funds.

Never invest any money
in the stock market that you
cannot afford to lose.

– Cuttie W. Bacon, III

Chapter 8

Stock and the Stock Market

Stock is ownership in a company. This ownership is evident by having a stock certificate as proof of ownership. Each unit of ownership is called a share. A person who owns a part of a stock company is called a shareholder or a stock-holder.

For the past five years owning the right stock has been an outstanding experience for millions of Americans. Many stocks have paid 20% or more and we constantly hear of people getting rich in the stock market. Because there is so much positive and negative publicity about the market, it is my belief that one needs a thorough orientation in the market before investing money. It is my advice to anybody who wants to invest in the stock market is not to invest any money that you cannot afford to lose.

The one question I am asked more than any is "What stocks should I buy?" My advice to everybody who wants to invest in the stock market it purchasing stock is as personal as buying your clothes. Since you do not ask people what you should wear and what you should buy, I think that anyone interested in investing in the stock market should research the market and get professional advise before investing any money. One should buy a stock by purchasing shares in a mutual fund company that invests in the stock market and relying on the expertise of professional fund managers to invest their funds for them.

For additional information, you can subscribe to my personal finance newsletter and attend seminars by calling Dr. Knose seminars, 1-800-995-9934. If you do not want to attend a class or seminar and get the basic information, I would recommend that you subscribe and read magazines like; *Money Magazine*, *Smart Money*, *Mutual Fund Magazine*, *Black Enterprise*, and other financial magazines that give good information on how to invest in the stock market. I would also recommend that you contact professional brokers like Jesse B. Brown; Author of *Investing in the American Dream*. A man with a proven track record, well established reputation, one who has been featured in the *Wall Street Journal* and one who has aided numerous people in developing their wealth in the stock market. I have met him and I believe he is one of the most skillful men in assisting people in building wealth in this country.

Dad earns his money,

Mother earns her money,

Make sure the children
earn their money.

– Cuttie W. Bacon

Chapter 9

Paycheck vs. Allowance

I t is a custom for parents at varying ages in their children's lives to decide that it is time to give them an allowance. I am opposed to the idea of giving youngsters an allowance because it has, in my opinion, no relationship to what life is about in the real world. In adult life, no one gives you money without receiving goods and services, in most cases. It is my belief that any money that children receive should be an opportunity to teach them a life long message on how money is acquired. It is my belief that when a child requests an allowance, it is time to begin to teach money lessons. I think the first money lesson a child should be taught is that money is exchanged for goods and services. When a child begins to ask for money it is time to find either goods or services that he or she can produce. It does not matter if the child is younger than 5 years old, but the lessons taught are most valuable. I suggest when it comes time to make a decision about money that you are going to give to children, sit with the child and decide what goods and services the child may exchange for money. A child 3 years old and older can be given the following responsibilities:

- Putting toys in their toy cabinet
- Picking up anything that is on the floor that should not be there
- Emptying small garbage cans
- Arrange books straight on the bookshelf

At 5 years old it is time to give more complex assignments to youngsters,

- Wiping and drying dishes
- Wiping off tables
- Assisting with small brothers and sisters
- Keeping all toys in their proper place

At 5 years to 8 years old they can begin to,

- Clean and shine shoes
- Wash and dry dishes

- Carry out garbage
- Assist in the cleaning of automobiles, bicycles, and other items around the house.

At 8 years to 12 they can,

- Start their own business
- Wash pots and pans
- Clean floors
- Operate garden equipment
- Assist in cutting grass and shoveling snow

Teaching youngsters the lessons of earning an allowance can be a preparation for adult life. I received my first lesson in earning my allowance at 10 years old. I requested my father to give me an allowance. At that time, he advised me that no young man that was worth his salt would sit around the house and expect his parents to give him money. He further advised me that if I wanted an allowance, the first thing I would have to do was earn it. This statement was very perplexing to me. I explained to my father that at 10 years old I knew that I could not get a job nor did I know of any jobs that would provide me the $2-3 dollars a day that I needed. My father, with a smile, explained to me that he would tell me of a business that I could make $2-3 a day. If I followed his instructions, he guaranteed me that I would always have money under his plan. The next day my father built me a wooden wagon about five feet long and two feet wide. He said this is your business. I want you to start a delivery service in the neighborhood. Go to each house within 3 blocks and tell everyone that you are the local delivery boy. Tell them when they need wood, ice, or coal, you would gladly go and pick it up and deliver it to them for a fee of 25-50 cents. This sounded like a very challenging business to me. My father was a very convincing man and I believed that I could be successful by following his recommendations.

I started my first business as he advised, and within 10 days, I was earning an average of $1.50 to $2.00 per day. After approximately 10 days, I was earning $3 in one day. When my father returned home from work I told him that my business was going well. His first question was how much did you make today? I said $3. He then asked where was the $3? I explained to him that I had bought candy and cookies and other junk food. He quickly explained to me that when I earned any money, my first obligation was to my mother to check and see if she needed any money to assist her in running the household. After checking with my Mom, I then had the freedom to do what I wanted. However, he strongly suggested that I save 25-50 cents per day. I did not agree with this recommendation, but it proved to be a very good one. Saving 25-50 cents per day allowed me, by age 16, to purchase my first used automobile – with cash.

These personal experiences reinforce my recommmendation that you find jobs for your children to do before they are adults. Issue an allowance to them in the form of a paycheck or encourage them to have employment outside the home. Assist them in managing the money they receive from these jobs. Under no condition should you give children money without attaching work or obligations to the money. If your child does not have an income or a job, issue IOUs until he or she gets a job or business. Then require them to pay on their IOUs every week.

Charging and keeping a
continuous balance of
$3,000 to $4,000 on five
charge accounts and making
your payments on time,
a person can give away more
than a half million dollars
in 25 years at 21% or more.

– Cuttie W. Bacon

Chapter 10

You Have Money to Invest Now, and You Don't Know It

After surveying a number of parents, I have found that many people have money that they can invest for their children, but because of poor planning and poor choices, most of this money is being wasted. In my surveys, I found that a typical Mother and Father who smoke a pack of cigarettes per day literally burn approximately $7 per day and $210 per month. Seven dollars per day invested for their child for 25 years in an investment of 15% or more would guarantee their child more than $588,271.

Liquor

Two parents who visit bars and have at least six Cocktails per week could result in more than $150 per month for drinks. These dollars could be used for sound investments for their child.

Designer Clothing

Designer clothing; shirts, pants and sweaters that cost in excess of $500 and can be bought for half that amount. I found that many people can invest more than $100 a month if they invest in ordinary garments rather than designer's garments. Children always outgrow garments until at least age 12. That expensive garment is left hanging in the closet drawing no interest. Imagine if it was $500 in Mutual Fund shares or a Certificate of Deposit?

Junk Food

My experience with junk food with my granddaughters has shown me that in a days time, you can spend $5-10 per child on junk food. If one bought healthy foods such as fruits and veggies, one could spend $1 per day in snacks for a child and invest $4-8 per day in sound investments to assist the child in becoming wealthy.

Cars

It is customary for upper and middle income people to drive expensive cars and frequently trade in those cars on more expensive cars. One of the worst investments one can make is to purchase a high priced luxury automobile. A new luxury car with all of the gadgets could cost as much as $50,000. At the end of two years, it is worth less than $30,000. It is much smarter to buy a well maintained two-year old car for $30,000 and invest the other $20,00 for your child. Because if you've noticed the stock market in the last five years, a person with an investment of $20,000 for his child in Microsoft stock would have $400,000 in approximately 5 years. Investing $20,000 every 4 years for a span of 12 years in stock that grew like Microsoft did from 1994-1999, a child would have more than a million dollars in a 12-year period. These kinds of investments for children are a much wiser investment than buying new luxury cars every few years.

In short, today, this very moment, you have numerous ways on cutting down on the amount of money that you are wasting. Making wise investments can lead to your child becoming a millionaire before he or she is 25 years old.

Another huge waste of money that 8 out of 10 middle income Americans have is credit cards. Charging $2,000 on a typical charge card and making every payment on time, a person today will pay an additional $8,000 over 8 years in addition to the $2,000 they charged. Unfortunately, many Americans have 4 – 5 charge cards with a similar balance of $2,000 or more and many will pay at least $8,000 per card over approximately 30 years to pay these accounts off. Five accounts at $2,000 at 21% or more will cost more than $40,000 over the next 30 years. Forty thousand dollars invested in stocks or mutual funds at 15% or more would result in $80,000 in 6 years.

Chapter 11

IRAs for Kids

What is an IRA?

An IRA is an individual retirement account. It is the only kind of tax advantage retirement account that can be opened by virtually anyone. You are allowed to contribute a maximum of $2,000 per year (as long as you earn at least $2,000 per year). The contributions may or may not be tax-deductible, depending on your level of earning and your marital status. The money will grow tax-free until you begin making withdrawals. If any money is withdrawn before the age of 59 1/2, the IRS will levy a 10% penalty on the money that is withdrawn.

What are the types of IRAs?

Deductive traditional IRAs, non-deductible traditional IRAs, and Roth IRAs. A deductible traditional IRA allows you to reduce your taxable income by the amount of the contributions to your IRA. A non-deductible traditional IRA, while not reducing your taxable income in the amount of your contributions, has no tax penalty on the earnings of the account until you begin to make withdrawals. A Roth IRA does not allow you to deduct contributions, but withdrawals that meet certain criteria are not taxed.

How Does an IRA Work?

A traditional IRA allows you to set aside money for retirement. The money is invested in any of a variety of vehicles – including stocks, bonds and mutual funds, sometimes determined by you and in other instances, decided by the institution at which the account is established. If you met certain income and other requirements, your IRA deposits become tax-deductible, reducing your taxable income dollar for dollar, and earnings on your IRA investments grow tax-free. However, your withdrawals will be taxed. In the Case of a non-traditional IRA or a Roth IRA, your contributions (or investments) to the IRA are not deductible, but you will not be taxed on the withdrawals.

How do you get one?

You can establish an IRA almost anywhere you want to. However, you should make sure you know what kinds of investments the financial institution allows its customers to make. Most IRAs are established at a bank, brokerage firm, mutual fund company, or insurance company. It is a good idea to find out if the institution allows you to invest your money in any manner you so choose or limits your selection or charges fees to invest your money in something other than what the institution itself offers.

How much does it take to start one?

A typical IRA can be established with as little as $50.

Are there restrictions on IRAs?

Yes, early withdrawal carries with it a penalty. The maximum amount that can be contributed in any year is $2,000.

I   Individual

R Retirement

A Account

What are the advantages?

The money grows tax-free until you begin making withdrawals. However, in the case of a Roth IRA that is used for certain expenses associated with higher education, early distributions may be tax-free and penalty-free. These expenses include tuition, fees, books, supplies, and room and board. While contributions to the Roth IRA are not tax-deductible, the principal and interest grow tax-free.

What are the disadvantages?

The limited amount of income you can invest each year and the penalty for early withdrawals may be considered disadvantages. Nevertheless, most financial consultants believe that some kind of IRA is a good buy for most investors.

Giving is one of life's
most precious experiences.

– Cuttie W. Bacon, III

Chapter 12

Giving, Tithing, and Prospering

The most significant lesson you can teach any child about being prosperous and becoming a millionaire is giving. It is significant to teach children giving lessons as early as 1 1/2 years old. Long before a child is truly clear on why he is giving gifts it should be a habit of his to give. Start a child out at 18 months old when you take him to a friend's house to visit. Give the child a gift to take to the person to give that he is visiting. As a child gets older, at 3 years, teach the child to give a gift to someone every day. If it is only a flower, a hand made card, or a positive compliment. By 4 years old when the child is clear on what giving is, teach him that for every significant day of the year, he should make a gift for the special people in his life. Start out with Mothers Day, Fathers Day, birthdays, anniversaries, Valentine's

Give so you may have
your needs met.

– Cuttie W. Bacon, III

Day, and special days in the lives of people in the family. Let the child know that these gifts do not have to be money. Some of the most precious gifts that people can receive are hand picked flowers, homemade Christmas cards, and handmade gifts. By 5 years of age, parents should be well underway in teaching a child to give gifts that are not material such as gifts of affection, gifts of love, gifts of kind words, gifts of appreciation, and gifts of praise. By age 5, parents should start teaching children to look for ways to always give, and to acquaint the child with the universal law of giving. That law is:

The more we give,
The more we will receive,
If we give unconditionally.

Teach your children about millionaires such as Rockefeller and others who gave away millions and always had millions. Teach them that the same law applies to them. If they give in abundance, they will always receive an abundance of everything they give.

An Example of Giving Millions

In all the research I have done on rich and wealthy people it has been consistently clear that

Give big so you
get big returns.

— Cuttie W. Bacon, III

giving has been an obsession with prospering in most millionaire lives. Andrew Carnegie was known as one of the few multi-millionaires, but was best known for giving away money. Carnegie was born into an impoverished family and obtained very little formal education. While working as a young messenger boy, he once returned $500 that he found that was equal to 10 years of his salary. In 1901 Carnegie sold his company for 400 million dollars. After he obtained the 400 million, he gave most of it away.

During most of Carnegie's life, he built more than 2,800 libraries for poor people and within one 10 year period in the early 1900's he gave away 350 million dollars.

An Example of Tithing

John D. Rockefeller was known to always tithe. From the days that he was making only $3.50 per week he religiously tithed and as his income increased he was always known to tithe. When millionaires were very few in this country, John D. Rockefeller became the first billionaire with an estimated wealth of 1.4 billion dollars. He was quoted as saying, "God gave him the

The highest level of giving
is for the joy you receive
in giving.

— Cuttie W. Bacon, III

power to make money." Newspaper accounts of John D. Rockefeller said that Rockefeller was the world's greatest giver.

It is significant to start children as young as age 2 to giving and tithing. I recommend this approach so that by the time a youngster truly understands what money is, by the teen years tithing and giving will be a lifestyle.

So I repeat to you to teach children to tithe, to tithe plus, and to give, give, and never stop giving. And to make their goal in life to be the same as Rockefeller who was known to be the world's greatest giver, then prosperity, millions, and billions will be theirs. Emotional, financial, spiritual and physical prosperity will be theirs in abundance.

The most important lesson to teach children is a spiritual prosperity consciousness. I have spent a considerable amount of time discussing material wealth and money but there is a difference between material prosperity and spiritual prosperity. Teaching children that the richest life is a life of spiritual prosperity and that understanding spiritual prosperity will allow them to have an abundance of everything that they need and

Never confuse
material prosperity with
spiritual prosperity.

– Cuttie W. Bacon, III

want in life. Having a clear understanding of a prosperity consciousness will enable children to grow and not become overly possessed with material things. Be confident that there is an abundance of everything we need as long as we trust, believe and understand spiritual prosperity is here for us.

Start thinking prosperously,

start acting prosperously,

and you will be prosperous.

And remember,
the choice is yours.

— Cuttie W. Bacon, III

Conclusion

I have spent a considerable amount of time on how to teach kids to be millionaires and I do believe that managing one's personal money and teaching money management at a young age is extremely important. But more important is to teach children the love for a spiritual being, the importance of wisdom and understanding, self respect, respect for others and the environment, how to tell and seek the truth at all times, how to respect oneself and others, and unconditional love for every man, woman, boy and girl.

Afterword

I want you to start today with the children in your life a plan for saving and investing. Whether it is 50 cents a day or a hundred a day, don't let a day pass without getting started. Whether it is a piggy bank, a bank savings account, or the place of your choice for saving, plan to start monthly investments for your child or children and encourage everyone in your child or children's life to join you in your plan. Remember, as little as one dollar a day from four relatives could amount to $150 a month, $1,800 per year, and more than a half million dollars before your child retires.

Call or e-mail me and let me know how you are doing a year from today at:

1-800-995-9934

or e-mail at Cuttie3@Compuserve.com

Bibliography

Ruff, Howard J. *"How to Prosper During the Coming Bad Years"* Times Books. 1979

Ponder, Catherine *"The Millionaire Moses"* DeVorss & Company. 1977

Merrill, Jean *"The Toothpaste Millionaire"* Houghton Mifflin Company. 1972

Stanley, Thomas J. Ph.D., and Danko, William D. Ph.D. *"The Millionaire Next Door"* Longstreet Press. 1997

Brown, Jesse B. *"Investing in the Dream"* Hyperion. 2000

Savage, Terry *"The Savage Truth on Money"* John Wiley & Sons, Inc. 1999

Powers, Mark J. *"Getting Started in Commodity Futures Trading"* Investors Publications, Inc. 1977

Robinson, Marc *"Basics of Investing"* Time Life Books, 1996

Chapman, Jack *"How to Make $1,000 a Minute: Negotiating Your Salaries & Raises"* Ten Speed Press. 1987

Bodnar, Janet *"Dollars & Sense for Kids"* Kiplinger Books, 1999

To have Dr. Bacon speak to your organization or to order any of his other products contact:

Dr. Knose Seminars
1-800-995-9934

or e-mail at
Cuttie3@compuserve.com

Financial Management

Prosperity Consciousness

Keynote Speaker

Cuttie W. Bacon III, Ph.D.

1-800-995-9934